AF379270

The Art of Law

Thomas William Winslow
Attorney and Counselor at Law

HERE I AM
PUBLISHING, LLC

Published by Here I Am Publishing, LLC.
780 Monterrosa Drive
Myrtle Beach, SC 29572
704-604-7265

ISBN: 978-1-958032-02-2

Book page composition by Levi Stephen

A product of the United States of America.

Dedication

This book is dedicated to my

- wife, Lauren, who is always there to support me as we work to support our community.

- children for whom I work to nurture my community so that my community can nurture them.

- parents who always served me so that I may serve God.

Acknowledgements

I acknowledge my team members at Winslow Law who give their hearts and souls to serve our clients, and I want to acknowledge our clients and community for trusting us to serve you.

Table of Contents

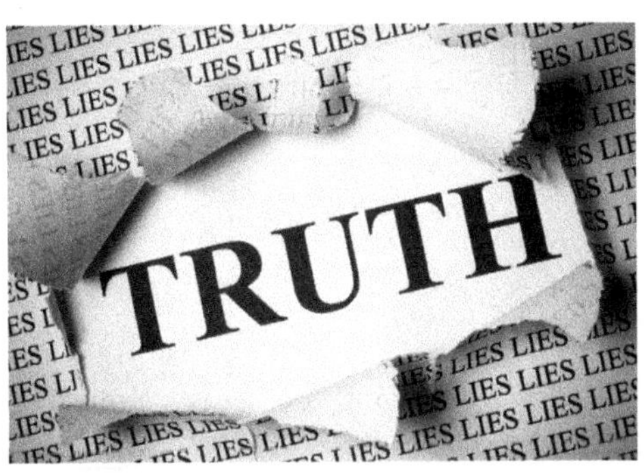

"And you will know the truth, and the truth will set you free."

—JOHN 8:32 (ESV)

INTRODUCTION

"You shall do no injustice in court. You shall not be partial to the poor or defer to the great, but in righteousness shall you judge your neighbor."

— Leviticus 19:15 (ESV)

It is said throughout law school that law is a practice; it is not art. But why is that?

- Is it because attorneys cannot get it right?
- Is it because attorneys need an excuse for unruly behavior?
- Is it called a practice due to the constant need to hone the craft and skill that is the advocacy of the law?

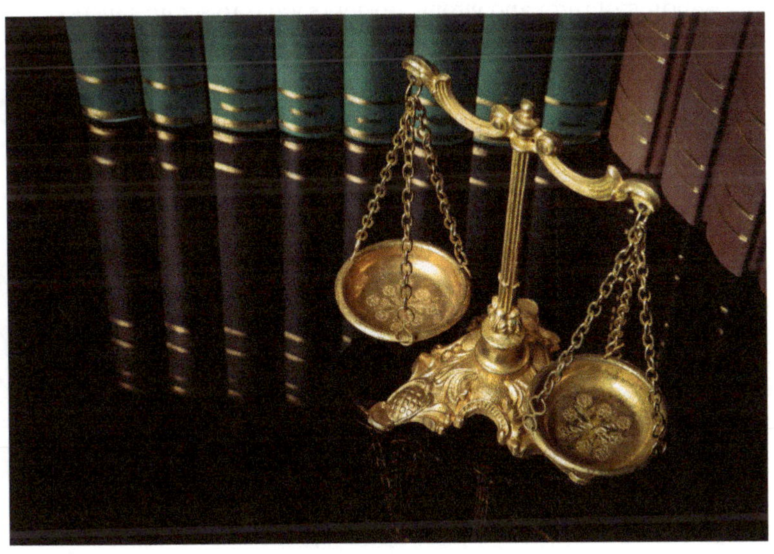

The truth is the advocacy accounts for only half the job of an attorney. The practice of advocacy is the attorney at law. But being the counselor at law is an art.

There is art behind everything we do in law and the way we perceive what is to come or what has already come. It is clearly important to our history, so we know what to expect in the future. It helps to build a perception of understanding—and of life—and of expectation. The art of law is understanding the perception of understanding all around you and interpreting that understanding to benefit those who hire us to represent them. To represent society, you must understand what society demands. Such a task is an art—and potentially the toughest art of all.

An attorney's goal should not be to win. An attorney's job is to balance justice in a society that craves a true understanding of right and wrong. Society's job is to set up a justice system in which attorneys, solicitors, counselors, ad litems, and/or anyone, including judges, deem it to be appropriate so the societal system is one that people find and believe is worth fighting for. When bad triumphs over good, when money flaunts the law, and when those charged with protecting justice disrespect the process, then being an officer of the court loses its purpose.

We must believe in the art of the law in an adversary system by showing it the respect it deserves and the civility the people need. Is it possible to understand what should be done when there is only one single person making that decision?

Is it a dictatorship where the judge or jurors act as an emperor(s) to issue the ruling? No, there should always be more than one perspective in the system, and we must respect each other's perspective, thus the crucial importance of multiple perspectives within a jury system.

CHAPTER I
PAINTING A PERSPECTIVE

"He recognized it and knew it. In others—clients, witnesses, or sometimes adversaries, he had seen or heard it: A gesture, a phrase, or a tone which exposed unintended truth in the beat of a second."

— JACKSON BURNETT, *THE PAST NEVER ENDS*

A perspective is an individual's accumulation of experience and education. It is not based on race, sex, creed, or wealth. It is based on life. Therefore, we have twelve jurors, not one. We have a panel of justices on the Supreme Court, not one.

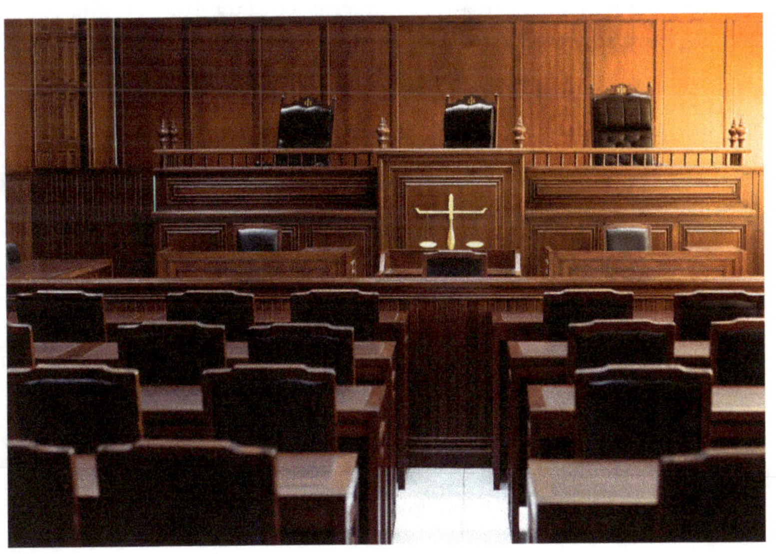

This is the reason the President of the United States does not make judicial decisions. It is that perspective that provides the societal role—not necessarily the counselors and attorneys. The counselors' and attorneys' jobs are to find the evidence that paints the picture behind the narrative being told.

That is the role of the attorney; that is the art of being an attorney. It is understanding the necessity of having the ability to paint a perspective of which more than one person would agree is correct. Every picture has an admirer; however, it is the masters who can create pictures that are amalgamations of many affirming perspectives.

Every day we practice because this is what we must do in order to perform at our highest level. Every sports team practices; every professional practices; every person practices something. But these are not practices of law. The art of law is what will differentiate you from all the others.

Practiced attorneys present themselves before a judge and jury much like artists present themselves on stage and perform before an audience. Much like an artist working on a canvas, the work of an attorney is not to only paint a picture, but also to bring sound, relativity, and life to the canvas. Not only do the jurors want to hear, but the jurors also want to issue an opinion. Why? Because you have painted a picture that has allowed them to visualize and not just hear a narrative. Your picture—your art—has touched many, if not all, of the five senses, thus, the jurors have experienced an unification of affirming perspectives and not just heard a litany of words.

If I were a blind-folded person standing in front of you holding an apple, how would you describe the apple for me? Is it a green apple or a red apple or a yellow apple? Does it have worm holes or is it bruised? Does it have a stem or not? How would you describe its taste? Is it tart, sweet, firm, or mushy? What sound might you hear if you bit into the apple? Would you hear a crunch? What would you like to do with the apple? Would you like to have an apple for yourself? Incorporating description—details—the five senses—will paint a more complete picture for the jurors.

Now, imagine I allow you to taste the apple. I allow you to smell it. I allow you to hear it as you bite into the fruit. As it turns out, I have a nice, firm, beautiful apple. Let us call it a Fuji apple straight from Japan. I am going to place that apple right into your hands. This is the kind of apple I would want served in a Dutch apple pie. You know the delicious dessert with the sugar cinnamon topping, with steam coming off the top as you pull it out of the oven. You go to the freezer and scoop out the vanilla ice cream. You cannot wait to grab your fork and get the first taste on your tongue.

That is art—painting your perspective so others can experience it by seeing it, tasting it, smelling it, hearing it, and touching it. Do not leave it up to the judge or jury to decide what kind of apple you have. It is up to you to paint your perspective. So, I have described my apple to you. I have laid out the picture for you to visualize. I have taken each piece of the puzzle and placed it where it belongs. This is art. This is the law.

As an attorney and an artist, we need the ability to gather all the evidence for the subject matter and then be able to put together all those various puzzle pieces to create a detailed picture, all the while performing in front of a judge, the jury, the client, and the adversary. Should we have a trial, hearing, or mediation? Whichever is the one, this is the show we are going to present to our audience. Our goal is to have our audience share a perspective that benefits us. This is the adversarial system that allows for the art of law to become a show. It allows for all members to describe what is going to happen and to put evidence into their own words by painting their own pictures to allow the audience members to close their eyes and see what is seen or heard or smelled or felt or tasted in each instance.

Thus, the benefit of the art of law is to show, not just to tell; it is to describe, not just to narrate; and it is to benefit all of society, not just yourself or your clients. The art of practicing law is to understand the perspectives that surround us and to be able to articulate that perspective in a civil manner that unites a group of people in a direction—like a jury or even society.

In summary, there are several **shoulds** that we must remember and strive to do each day.

- We **should** always work to understand other perspectives, not just our own.
- We **should** always try to describe a case from every side.
- We **should** utterly understand the perspectives surrounding that one fact, which can change the entire case—the perspectives surrounding your client and the other side's client.

What are the perspectives that matter to you?
  • To the other side?
  • To the jury?
  • To the third party who does not care?
  • To the third party who doesn't want to be there?

What is the description of your case that truly, truly matters?

This is the art of practicing law. Now, let us explore the art of law and try to understand what behooves our clients and society to find the true justice that is demanded.

Chapter II
The Art of Knowing Yourself

"The glory of justice and the majesty of law are creed not just by the Constitution—nor by the courts—nor by the officers of the law—not by the lawyers—but by the men and women who constitute our society—who are the protectors of the laws as they are themselves protected by the law."

—Robert Kennedy

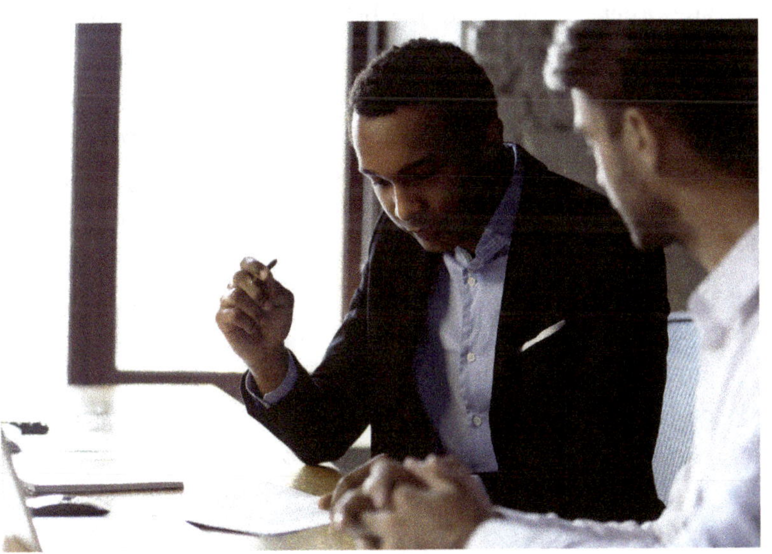

Anytime you reflect upon the art, the first thing that must be done is to reflect upon yourself. To understand the art of law is to understand

- who you are,
- who your firm is,
- who your paralegal is, and
- who your staff is.

To paint a picture you must understand the materials you will need to reflect the picture you want to show. Far too many in law school and other professional schools only reflect upon the study, the history, and the understanding of what something is. In law school, they never teach you to understand what kind of lawyer you will be or who you will become as an attorney. The same thing is true in any other school, including business schools or even art schools. Very rarely do they teach you what kind of art you are going to be reflecting upon. Study might focus on the arts of the past, but why not study the people you will be working for or the benefit you will be to society? If all of these elements were considered, it would take far too long for many professionals to understand the intricacies of their field.

That is why you hear people complain they are burned out. You have to have time to reflect upon what kind of professional you are going to be and what kind of lawyer you are going to be. It is not until you utterly understand yourself that you can be a true professional and reflect the art of your business.

For way too long, professionals, such as myself, have tried to emulate those who surround them:
- "Well, you should do it this way."
- "You should not do it that way."
- "Go watch someone and see how he/she does it."

Many young individuals take these suggestions as instruction to mean you should be like another person. But that is not what these suggestions mean. These are examples of what you could be.
- Do your actions reflect how you feel?
- Do you channel that energy?
- Are you a Van Gogh?
- Are you a Picasso?
- What kind of artist are you?

When you can reach an understanding and express the kind of artist you are, then you will not burn out.

In law, 60% of attorneys are introverts (www.abajournal. com). Such facts beg the question, should they be litigators in front of a jury? Probably not. Does that mean introverts cannot be litigators? No, introverts can be litigators, but they have a completely unique style, different from the style extroverts have. Let us examine this closer.

1. Do they put on a show?
2. Do they state the facts the same way that an extrovert does?
3. How do they tell their stories so a judge and jury and clients will believe them?

4. What is it about them that reflects the art they want to show?
5. Are they realists?
6. Are they abstract artists?
7. What is it they do that not just says but shows and creates a picture using all five senses?

By examining others as people you deem to be introverts, you can gain insight and knowledge that will help you apply these questions to yourself and assist you in determining more about who you are.

The first step you must take is to reflect upon yourself concerning what kind of artist you will be. Next, you must understand your studio. Your studio is your firm; your studio is your office.

- Does your firm reflect who you are?
- Does your office reflect who you are?
- Does the team show your clients the kind of person you are?
- Do you have professional and personal items on display?
- Do you have a Bible? Do you have a libations bar? Do you have both?

What kind of image are you trying to exhibit? What is your costume?

- Do you wear a three-piece suit?
- Do you wear a white shirt, a flannel shirt, shorts, flip-flops, expensive watch, no watch?
- What kind of image are you portraying?

- What kind of car do you drive?
- What do you look like?
- What is your persona?
- Who do you represent?
- Who are you to your clients and to your adversaries?
- Who are you to society in general?
- Do you reflect what you want to reflect to
  the community?
- Do you keep your hair cut?
- To whom do you appeal?
- Do you drive a motorcycle?
- Do you drive a truck?
- What are you?
- Are you submerged into who you want to be, and do you fully accept who you want to be, or are you still conflicted about who you want to be and who you want to appeal to?
- Do the people around you reflect the image you want to reflect? Your paralegal? Your receptionist? Your legal staff? Your courier who delivers things to your office?
- Do your children, your spouse, and your loved ones reflect the images you reflect?

If you genuinely want to be an artist in the art, you must submerge yourself in the art. You have to understand that without 100% dedication, it is not art; it is a hobby, or it is simply a paycheck. You are practicing—we do not want to practice; we are making art. We are going to focus on creating an image that reflects the picture we want to be perceived as having. Only when you can understand the image you want to be, then others can, as well.

It is important for your team to understand that through policies and procedures, you put into place the guidelines you have regarding the wardrobe, rules, and benefits you have. Everything matters, even down to the way your team answers the phone, the way they respect and give clients care, and the way they treat opposing counsel.

It is important to accept the reputation you want to parlay, for if you cannot accept it yourself, others will not accept you for whom you pretend to be. Ask yourself if you are pretending to be someone who you are not? Are you really giving your best effort, or is it simply something or someone you have been told you should be like?
- Believe in yourself.
- Believe in your image.
- Believe in who you are.
- Have confidence, not cockiness.
- Accept that you are not perfect.
- Accept that you are who God made you to be.
- And honestly accept that not all people will accept you for who you are, and be okay with that. This is confidence.

But you do not want to become overly confident and believe everyone should be just like you or that you are better than others if they are not like you. That is cockiness because the truth of real diversity is not based on gender or skin tone or any other natural changes we have amongst ourselves. But true diversity is that we accept others for how God made them—not how they have chosen through their "free will" to act. No matter what gender or skin tone or age you are, you can choose to act a certain way; you can choose your behavior; and you can choose your attitude.

There is nothing wrong with personality because each different personality appeals to a different audience. It appeals to potentially different adversaries or even clients, but it is not until you accept that and accept there are other types of perspectives and personalities out there that you truly accept the art of being a professional. It is the art of creating relationships and the art of law.

Create relationships by being who you are and accept others for whom they are. It is amazingly simple, but that is how you form life-long relationships—not just a perception that you want their money, or you want to win. You may win or get the money once, but you may never see that person again. When you create a relationship, it does not matter how much you charge. Sometimes, whether you win or lose, the client, the adversary, the judge, and/or the jury will all understand you and what you are trying to portray. By reflecting who you truly are, everyone around you will also accept who you truly are and will want to work with you again.

Step number one of perfecting the art of law is to understand who you are, reflecting on who you truly are so that others around you will accept and create a relationship with you. You cannot do that until you understand yourself and you understand that everything around you—from your car to your furniture, to the way you dress, to your staff, to your family and friends—must reflect that same image. If they do not, then the client and anyone else will notice the inconsistencies and will not truly accept you for who you are, resulting in your credibility and reputation suffering. If you do not put down your shield or you cannot influence others to put down their shields, then no others can create the relationships with you that you hope to create with them, which are true, sustainable relationships. That applies to client, co-workers, and even your families.

To have a real relationship you must be authentic and accept the authenticity of those with whom you surround yourself.

Chapter III
The Art of Knowing Your Mind

"It's every lawyer's dream to help shape the law, not just react to it."

— Alan Dershowitz

Being a professional and an attorney is not simply about the ability to exude that of understanding and confidence in what we do. It is about being able to manage mentally what we have to do. As a professional, an attorney's art of law is the art of professionalism. It is important how we learn to cope with the

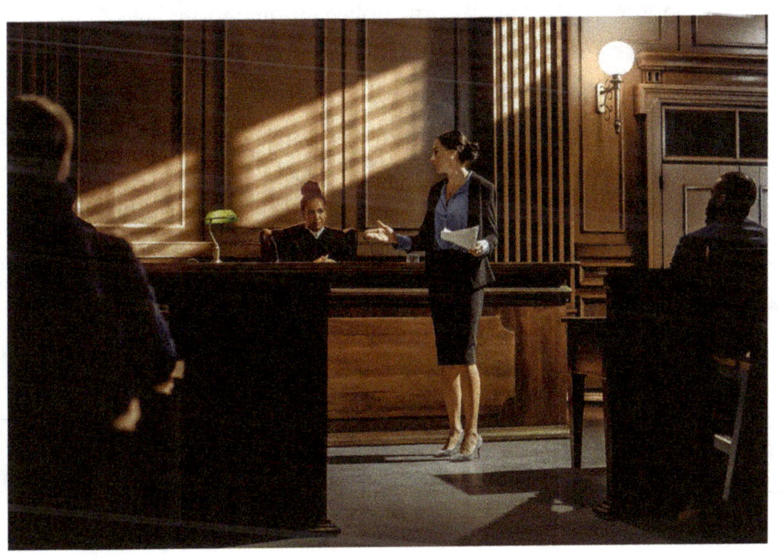

pressures and stresses placed upon us. I cannot think of another profession where there are more jokes about the job. Yet there are those of us who desire to become the butt of these jokes, literally going to school for a multitude of years and spending a multitude of money to be someone else's punchline.

Why do this to ourselves? Because no matter the number of jokes there are about attorneys, it is still a respected profession that can make a difference in other people's lives and in society as a whole. Every profession is going to have its bad apples. It is the outliers who are just not good examples of the profession. Do not be one of the outliers. Do not become one. Do not act like one. Understand that everything you do is a representation of the level of respect the profession has built up for over a millennium. As attorneys, it is our job to enforce those laws that have been created.

Some might say, "But the police enforce those laws." No, the police merely arrest the perpetrators opposing the law. The attorneys enforce the laws. The attorneys are the ones who decide the amount of punishment or if there is going to be punishment for those violations.

And as such, how do you cope with the stress of asking to end a man's life on a death penalty case? How do you cope with seeing children taken from their parents because their parents do not know how to manage a situation? How do you watch people being divorced day in and day out? Or how do you witness those cases where families have lost loved ones from the negligence of others?

The list goes on, considering the plethora of vices that enter in a courtroom: those who have lost the ability to create a living due to bad workplace situations; those who have lost family members; or those who have lost monetary value due to corrupt organizations.

As attorneys, we are forced into situations where we must represent people we would not naturally want to represent, but we are under obligation from the court and assigned that job of representing someone for free just because the court wants us to.

There are the day-in and day-out calls from clients who cannot afford us, asking us to represent them for free. Consider the times when we also are known as attorneys who cannot afford to work for free in order to keep our businesses running. We also have the obligation to the law and to the court to do what is best for society—not just for ourselves.

Are you appointed by the court to work Pro Bono, or do you simply do it for the benefit of society?

Every day, attorneys carry an obligation on their shoulders to do what is best for society. Yet, we are the butt of jokes because of those who do not agree with us and decide to disrespect us rather than to understand us.

As an attorney or as a paralegal or as just yourself, you must decide whether you can manage that situation. And when you cannot manage such burdens, you are sure to face burnout. But before that occurs, you may have a situation of depression or addiction, perhaps alcoholism. That is why there are so many attorneys or people in the law who are addicted to substances because they need a source of relief—relief that momentarily removes those burdens and stressors from their shoulders.

Perhaps they never considered how the reality of each day would be before they entered the profession. Perhaps they had never created mechanisms to release and relax—ways of supporting themselves or having others support them. Staunch support mechanisms might be our spouses, our families, or faith. We must fall back on these support mechanisms and allow them to do what they are supposed to do. Attorneys must realize they are not stronger than the entire weight of the law on their shoulders. They are not able to cope with the pressures that will be upon them alone. And as those who are already in the field know, when you leave work at the end of the day, the day is seldom over. The cell phone will ring, the court will call, the law shows on TV will pester, and the friends at a party will ask legal questions. We are never free from the glorious responsibilities and privileges of representing those we have chosen to serve. These are not burdens or situations of deficit. Indeed, we receive a benefit unlike any other benefit.

We have received what we might refer to as a calling and in response, we have dedicated our lives to the law and society so we can help people. We cannot walk away from it, but if and when we do, this is referred to as burnout or retirement. It is probable that even in retirement, we will be approached about the law. Instead of trying to flee from it or experience burnout, rejoice in the fact that we have been given this unique privilege and have this ability, which few others have. We are in such high demand that no matter where we go, people need us.

Accept the fact society needs us. Accept the fact we have a role that is greater than ourselves. It is not about us. It is not about having enough money, having enough power, or having enough for ourselves. Those are individualistic measures. Accept the fact you are not enough, and you, alone, cannot do what needs to be done in the legal field to create justice, freedom, and liberty.

This becomes our daily struggle, our daily grind—in and out every day. Rejoice for those who are not burdened with this stress. Those who do not perform the work do not possess the responsibilities we have. God has not blessed them with the same position. He has blessed us with the ability to assist others in situations where they cannot help themselves.

Very rarely do clients, other individuals, or other attorneys approach us unless they need something from us. "I can handle this myself." Very rarely do we ever hear those words uttered from people in our office. If they are able to handle the situation without us, then we do not have jobs or clients. So, recognize their inability and need as a glorious responsibility we have been chosen to do and one we have chosen to take upon ourselves.

We have been given this privilege—our profession and what we do—by God. Some of us may not believe we possess the demeanor or the ability, but rest assured, there is a place for us in the law. We all have our own place. We need to discover what our place is. Once we find our place, we need to determine how to best manage it.

We need to find our mechanisms for release, such as practicing meditation, participating in physical activities, spending time with our families, listening to music, or even acting. When you need to de-stress, choose your mechanism because if you do not find your healthy resource for stress release, then an unhealthy mechanism will choose you. That may be the inability to cope through suicide, drinking, or drugs. All of these bad choices offer a false sense of security for you.

Those false mechanisms will never be enough because we forfeited control in choosing them; we allowed them to choose us. Whenever something chooses you, you become a different person. You are not truly who you think you are. Select the mechanism that releases the level of stress you are experiencing, so you are truly who you think you are. If not, you will eventually lose the battle, so free your mind and body as soon as you have the opportunity. Why? Because right around the corner is a need for which you will be called.

We need to be in the best shape possible to manage the situation for the person who needs us. We cannot be concerned about ourselves. It is time to be concerned about the person who has called upon our services. This is why we must have found our place, so we will be in a condition to handle his/her need.

Chapter IV
The Art of Knowing the Answer

"A lawyer's time and advice are his stock in trade."

— Abraham Lincoln

To be able to understand one's own position in one's own mind permits the person to have confidence in his/her own ability to face an adversary.

Once we understand our abilities, we will be able to know what our true gifts are and what skills we need to hone. Each of us will discover a unique skill we possess that can

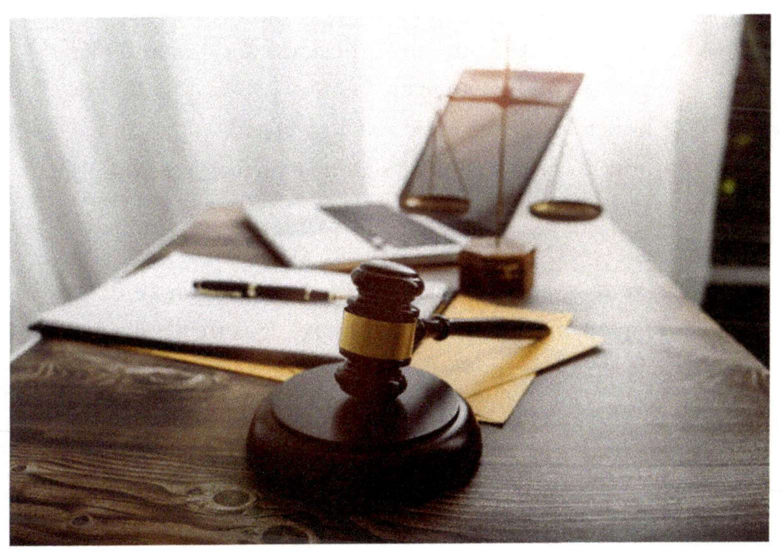

contribute to a team. Why? Because we cannot do it alone. Teams are vital to us. It is always foolish to believe we can do everything ourselves.

If we believe we are perfect in everything we do, then the downfall of micromanaging will arise. We cannot do everything, so the sooner we accept this reality, the sooner we will be able to achieve what we are destined to accomplish.

The problem is that too few understand they cannot do it all, and too many think they cannot do anything at all. It is those in the middle who truly succeed. To micromanage simply means you do not trust those around you. To not have a team simply means you are too egotistical to understand you need someone to help you in your weaknesses. But once you are able to recognize the issue and have that team in place, you need to discover their vital roles. Very few people understand

- all there is to know about business and law and marketing and human resources.
- how to be an attorney and a paralegal.
- how to be a customer service manager, receptionist, and a legal administrator.

If we take on all of these roles, if we take on all of the roles of a law firm, then we either have egos that believe we can do it all, or we do not have enough assets to accomplish what it is we need to do. As a result, we will lack an efficiently run business and will not have enough time to serve our clients, our co-workers, and ourselves. It is important for us to remember our law firm is not designed for us. It is not designed for us to make money. It is not designed for us to have more and more and more.

Our law firm is designed for us to provide services for our clients—what they have paid us to provide. The true understanding of the law is service that benefits the client—not us. We will never see a quarterback without an offensive line. We will never see a coach without a team. No CEO has time to manage a business and manage all its cases alone.

Our clients are looking for someone who can provide them with answers. Do we have all the answers they need? Probably not. We need to comprehend their problem first, thus the importance of listening. We cannot be experts in every field of law. We cannot know the answer to every question. We should never be ashamed to say, "I do not know," or "I need to research that."

We must be able to investigate the law. We cannot be too lazy to use the tools and resources, which are available around us. We are paid to provide a solution—the best solution. I can promise you the answer is out there.

We are not paid to compound a problem. We are simply paid to assist those with a problem they already had. If we do not provide a solution, we are of no benefit to them. Understand a solution is within our grasp. Too many times attorneys turn away cases because they do not know the answer. But if they did know the answer, their declining of cases was probably due to boredom or fear of damage to their reputation.

The fun part of being an attorney is knowing how to find the answer, sort of like being a detective. That is what law school is about: to teach us how to find the answer. If there is no answer, that is when we have a novel situation that we help create an answer, thus providing for others in the future. This is the beauty of the law. We can actually assist in creating answers.

We get paid for our time, and we get paid for our efforts, but each of those — time and effort — feed our ultimate goal. We get paid for our opinions, literally our opinions. They may not even be fact. They may simply be how we feel based on our training and experience. How many fields get paid for giving an opinion about how they feel in the situation? Not many, I can assure you. I pay an accountant to prepare my taxes, not to simply have an opinion about them.

We give opinions based on our diligent research. As mentioned earlier, there is no shame in saying, "I don't know." But never tell a client you do know only to return to the client and confess you do not know. If you cannot find an answer, tell the client, "I am sorry. I cannot find the answer. However, based upon my education, knowledge, and experience, I am able to give you an opinion as to the best course of action." We should never lead a client astray if we just do not know. The client is counting on us. Never devalue opinions by issuing a guess.

The course depends upon your field. It will not be the same course of action for tax, probate, civil, criminal, family, or social security disability. Each and every field will require a different opinion. We have to be able to find our field in which we are knowledgeable. There is nothing wrong with general practice, but we better have people who have specialized knowledge in all the various fields for which we intend to provide an opinion.

If we do not have knowledge in those fields and we are unwilling to work to find an honest answer, then we should not be giving someone an opinion and getting paid for it. That is purely fraud. We are not benefiting that person; we are benefiting ourselves. We are giving the person bad information for good money, and that is not what we are paid for.

Chapter V
The Art of Knowing Your Client

"We educated privileged lawyers have a professional and moral duty to represent the underrepresented in our society, to ensure that justice exists for all, both legal and economic justice."

— Sonia Sotomayor

In the art of law, the clearest competition is that of opposing counsel. However, to think the opposing counsel is our competition is the immediate fallacy in the law. The true

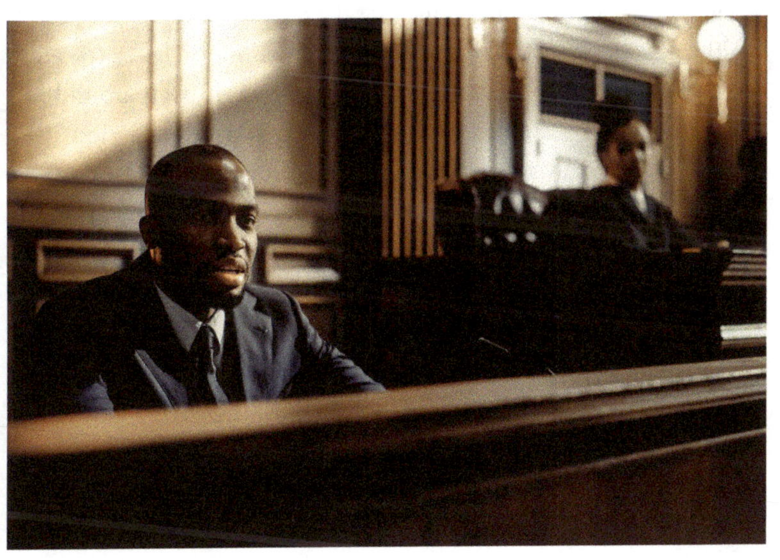

competition, in many cases, are our clients. It might seem weird that our interests are not absolutely aligned with our clients' interests. It might seem crazy to think we may not see things the same way as our clients, since they are paying us to represent their interests; however, most of the time, clients' interests are based upon emotion, which is what clouds their ability to remedy the situation on their own. If they did not have the emotion caught in the decision-making process and were able to think logically, many times they would be able to come to a resolution without us being a part of it. Unfortunately, many cannot get past their own personal feelings to be able to think of the transaction as a business transaction. Thus, our role as attorney—thus, our role as a paralegal—thus, our role as a firm—thus, our role as a whole—is impossible to resolve situations short of jury or judge decisions without removing the emotion and evaluating the risk/benefit scenario of every transaction. Be it contract liability or even simply disability, there is no way around understanding emotion and its correlation with resolution.

Once again, the art of the law is to remove the emotion and to think logically like we have been trained to do. It does not matter what our emotions are or what our clients' emotions are. And now we have a clearer picture as to why our biggest adversaries many times are our own clients. Many of them come to an attorney, wanting a pit bull, wanting a bulldog, and wanting someone to fight for them.

Fighting is an emotion. No one who has ever thought logically about a situation has ever thought that the first thing to do is to throw punches. This is not the best resolution because at the end of the day, everyone gets hurt in a fight. Even the winner gets hurt. He/She is out of time. He/She is out of money. More often than not, sometimes there is a draw. There is a mistrial; there is a hung jury. We have to fight again. And yet there remains no resolution because of the emotions controlling the situation. Where is the return on investment in that situation?

Now, do not get me wrong. There are times when logically we must fight. And logically there is no resolution short of trial with a judge or a jury verdict. We need the decision of a third party; yet, as an attorney, this is not the first reaction we should have. The art of law is to listen to our clients, to hear what they want, and to assess one simple question: What are the goals the clients want to achieve? The sole goal is not to win. That is not a goal that is a final position.

- What is it they want to win?
- Why do they want to win?
- Who do they want to win that from?

Once you understand what the goal is, then ask yourself, what is your role in achieving the goal? Because even though they have a goal, we might not have a role in it, and they do not even realize that. Or, although we have a role, we might not share their goal. Do not enter into a situation thinking you know what the goal is.

Remember, this is not our case as an attorney; this is our client's case. Are we working for ourselves, or are we working for our clients? A true advocate works for whom he/she is advocating—not for himself/herself. It is not about the money and getting as much money as you can. It is about providing our clients with solutions that achieve their goals. We cannot understand what the solution is unless we understand what the problem is. Our job is to set a path and to set a course to achieve their goals. Knowing our role is to drive to the goal. It is our role to listen, but it is our clients' roles to navigate to their goals with our advice.

What is it we are to do in every scenario? What is it we are supposed to be doing when we are achieving their goal? How do we achieve that goal? How do we achieve what it is that we are supposed to be doing? That is the importance of our role as an attorney, but how do we understand that unless we are listening to our clients, being an attorney, and being a counselor at law?

If we are not a counselor first, we cannot be an attorney second. If we do not listen, how do we know what to say? Yet in law school, no one teaches the counseling part. Rarely do we see *Attorney and Counselor* signs anymore. We see *Attorney at Law*. How is it that our legal profession has forgotten its primary role is to be a counselor to those who need legal help?

You are a counselor.

Much like a medical counselor or any other kind of counselor, we make a diagnosis, and we prescribe a remedy. We diagnose the legal issues they have, and we prescribe the legal remedies, which are available. Sometimes, there are no legal remedies, and it is our job to tell them there are no legal remedies. That does not mean that our role as an attorney ends; it means that our job now is to mitigate the damage that is going to occur due to the legal issues. Understanding that our role is vital to understanding their goal is the first step in achieving a true remedy to the problems they have. After all, you are a Doctor of Law.

There is no way to assess a proper legal remedy without understanding the goal of your client. To walk into a meeting or walk into any scenario and think you know what needs to be done is like a medical doctor walking into an appointment for a minute or two, hearing a cough, and diagnosing a cold. You are not taking the time to understand the true symptomology and the impact it has in that person's life. To prescribe the proper course of action, do not enter the legal field thinking that you are doing it for yourself or thinking that you are doing it for more money.

Remember, you are entering the legal profession to help those people in front of you. You need to assess the situation by removing the emotion and entering into a logical course of action that will fulfill the obligation set before you. The first step in removing emotion is simply listening to the clients and understanding you are not their cheerleader; you are their attorney. Whether it is good, bad, or ugly, it is your job, your role as an attorney, advocate, or counselor to simply tell them the truth.

Your role is to tell the clients clearly what can and cannot be done. You have a moral and ethical code to speak that truth. Do not hide it, do not lie to the clients, and do not be afraid of what may be prescribed because you know you are prescribing it for their benefit. You are there to help provide the solution. You will walk with the clients every day through that course.

Once again you are an attorney, not a cheerleader. But you are also your client's coach. You make the game plan, and you help to facilitate it. You are a player coach. You are the quarterback, and you may need the client to help you. You need help answering questions, taking depositions, or obviously assisting at a trial. You are setting that course, and if you are not willing to step up and do what is necessary to set that course, then clearly you are not the proper attorney for your client or that situation.

To attack the problem, sometimes we must attack the clients — not physically, of course. Do we tell them they are right when they are wrong? Do not hide what needs to be exposed, and do not expose what needs to be hidden. We do have an obligation, and we have client-attorney privilege. Understand the rules and understand the goals. But primarily, the art of law is being able to control our own clients. If we cannot control our clients, our clients will control us. Then we have already lost in the battle of emotion. There will never be a logical conclusion beyond pure winning. Nowhere in law does anyone purely win due to the time and money involved in every scenario.

Chapter VI
The Art of Knowing the Opposing Party

"One of the things I was taught in law school is that 'I'd never be able to think the same again'—that being a lawyer is something that's part of who I am as an individual."

— Anita Hill

Once we understand ourselves and we understand our clients, it is time to understand our opposing counsel because, truthfully, our opposing counsel has the same issues as we do.

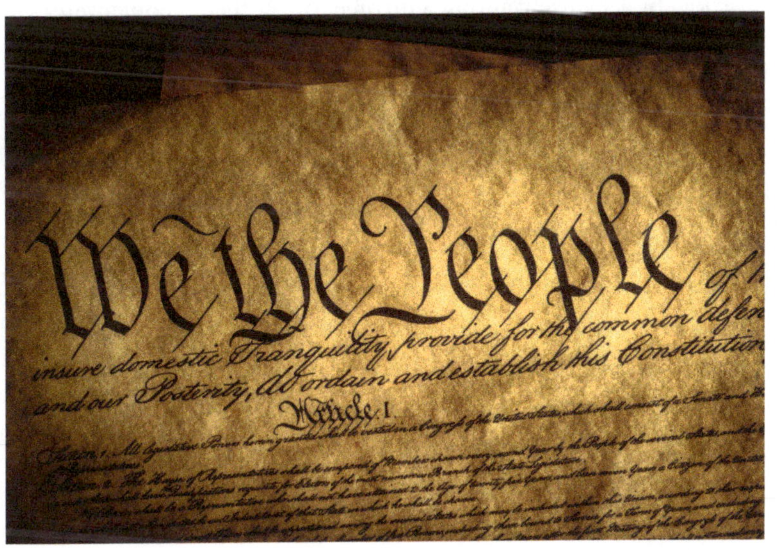

- They must understand themselves.
- They must understand the law.
- They must have a team around them whom they trust.
- They must deal with their own clients.

So, to understand the opposing counsel, we must first understand their client. Analyze the client and what the client is looking for. Analyze the goal of their client because many times the opposing counsel and people on the other side do not take on the same process as we will by understanding the art behind the law.

Many people in the legal world have not taken time to understand the goals; they may not even understand their role. So, analyze the client on the other side (and there is always a client). The client may be an insurance company, a corporation, or a spouse wanting a divorce. But if these people were your clients, what would their goals be? That is something to expose and investigate even during a deposition. Analyze who the client is. What is the client looking for? How can we help the client achieve it?

Why would we want to help the opposing counsel's clients achieve what they are wanting? Because sometimes simply by understanding what it is the other party wants to achieve, we can actually achieve our own client's goals, as well. Many people immediately believe the goal of the other side is to screw them, so they get nothing, so they achieve nothing, so they lose everything, such as a spouse fighting over every little thing or the insurance company in a car accident wanting them to get nothing. I rarely find this to be true.

More likely than not, especially with an insurance company, they are measuring risk.

For the right amount of money, they will pay it even for a situation they know they are not responsible. Why? Because the cost of doing business is going to be more beneficial when they can offer to settle the case instead of litigation. It may just be a $5,000 offer even though you knew you were not going to file the case because you analyzed the client on the other side and that insurance company has decided that paying you or not paying you is how to reduce its risk of getting out of the case as quickly as it can.

The same thing occurs with spouses: many times, men are okay with providing their spouses the necessities they will need to survive; they just do not want to be burdened with a lifetime of alimony or even child support. Women, on the other hand, oftentimes want that security of the lifelong gift of alimony. Alimony is an inherent situation that leaves nobody happy, but by understanding that, many times you can find a compromise, such as a temporary alimony or rehabilitative alimony, which provides them the confidence and the money to come to a point where they are okay not having that lifelong legal gift/obligation placed upon them.

It is important to understand our opposing party before we understand opposing counsel. When we take the opposition's depositions, do not just ask them about the situation.

- Ask what led up to the situation.
- Ask about moving forward in the situation.
- Ask what they are looking for.
- Ask why they are suing.

Dig deeper by asking why they are suing your party. Explore the motives behind the situation, not just the situation itself. Further, investigate the people themselves. Do they have assets because if they have assets, they are likely not looking for money no matter how they try to play it? Are they looking for money because they do not have any assets? Are they starting a new job in another city or state, and they want to get out of town quickly? Maybe time is the most important thing to them. Are they in a new relationship, and they just want to get it over with no matter what the stakes may be?

Understand that our opposing parties have their own goals, and they may not be the same as those of their counsel. By understanding both parties and their separate goals, we can fill in the role that their attorney should be filling in. If their attorney is not filling the role the client wants, that client will naturally cling to you if you can provide him/her with the desired goal.

For example, if an insurance company's attorney just wants to fight and spend money, but you show the other party's clients an avenue to resolution, they will lean towards you and benefit you as you move forward in the case. This happens many times in mediation if you can gain their trust. Once you gain the trust of the opposing party, then you can drive the ship by being the advocate and not the enemy.

There is a lot more benefit to being civil, polite, and looking for a resolution as opposed to being adversary and looking for a fight. Nobody wins in a fight, but everybody wins in a consented resolution. Look at how the opposing party dresses. Look at how the opposing party holds themselves.

Notice the demeanor they have in a deposition. Consider their confidence level by critiquing their handshakes when leaving a meeting. Consider their conceit level. How are they playing to a jury or even a judge?

The same analysis we do with our own clients, we must do with the opposing party. Always analyze who they are and what they are. This goes for their witnesses, as well, for the story of a client is merely that: it is the text in a book. The witnesses are the characters in that book who help provide the illustrations. But are the witnesses believable? Are the witnesses presentable? What level of cockiness or confidence do they have? Can they actually achieve the goals the attorney claims they can achieve? If we do not think they can, we must have the confidence ourselves to call them out on that. This is not practice; it is art. We must be able to read a book, paint a picture, and have the picture felt through emotions within the story. So, paint the picture the best you can paint, but by painting that picture, you must understand the client, the opposing client, and the witnesses. Once you understand these three, then you can analyze all the evidence.

Each piece of evidence is a piece of a puzzle. We put them all together to create a picture. Sometimes that picture is ugly, and that is when we know we need to settle a case. Sometimes that picture is beautiful; that is when we know we can go to trial. Sometimes, the picture is missing pieces. That is when the case is worthless. It happens, but we need to be honest about it and not lie to ourselves or our clients. It is simply a risk/benefit analysis. To the insurance company that has a lot of risk, the company may be willing to settle the case because of that situation. So, do not be afraid to analyze all parties, all witnesses, all evidence, and put your picture together. Once you have your picture together, you know the quality and the value of your art.

- Can you hang that picture on the wall?
- Would you hide it in the closet?
- Is it time to push this case as hard as you can?
- Is it time to settle this case?
- Is it time to take what you can get?
- Is it time to roll the dice?

Honestly, you should feel as confident as the other side. That is what builds leverage. Either they have leverage on you once you paint the picture, or you have leverage on them.

I understand that no one has ever come to an attorney, an insurance adjuster, a judge, a mediator, a client, or an opposing client because the person is just not smart. Everyone has intelligence; everyone is smart in what he/she knows. It might only be in this person's own perception, but if you treat the client as if the client is dumb because he/she does not see it the way you see it, then you are acting against yourself and against your client's best wishes. Understand, people have a different perception of the same picture. Not everybody likes Van Gogh and not everybody likes Picasso, but they are both considered masters. Just because a master artist created the picture does not mean it is going to sell. Just because you think it is ugly, does not mean it is worthless to somebody else.

It is all about perception and understanding the goals of the parties around you. Do not undervalue and do not overvalue; just simply value and try to get as many different diverse perceptions of the same picture as you can to pursue with opposing counsel and/or opposing parties.

Chapter VII
The Art of Knowing the Opposing Counsel

"People are getting smarter nowadays; they are letting lawyers, instead of their conscience, be their guide."

—Will Rogers

If we are fortunate enough to understand the opposing party as much as we understand our own clients' goals, then we have an advantage immediately over the opposing counsel. The advantage is not to be rubbed in their faces. The advantage is not to be used as a personal weapon; it is simply leverage for

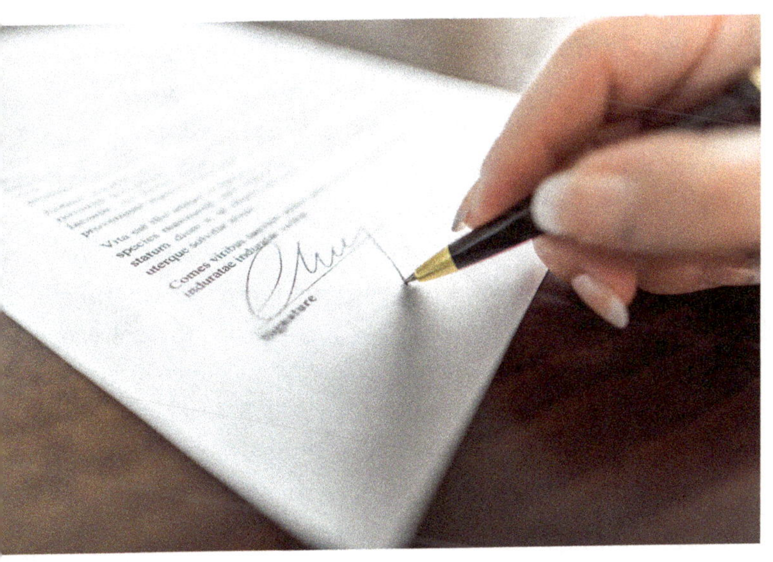

us to resolve the case. We should work hard to use it in civil accord and cooperation with our opposing counsel.

The opposing counsel is no longer our foe. Understand that opposing counsel is our friend, so treat him/her as such. We both have the same goal and that is to resolve the case. How we resolve the case may differ, but until such a time as it is clear we cannot resolve it amicably, why not work together to try to create a win/win situation?

All the way through trial, we can still be civil; however, we do have a duty to defend our clients, and we do have a duty to defend ourselves from the behaviors and tactics of some attorneys. Very rarely do any of us find a positive outcome develop naturally from an enemy. As such, always try to keep opposing counsel as a friend. Keep him/her close and ask about family, work, and everything there is to know about this person. Understand this person. What makes him/her happy? What makes him/her tick? And also understand the person has a job to do. Nothing the opposition does should be personal, and nothing you do should be personal. You both have a job to achieve, but what is that job? Does opposing counsel understand that job is not to win? Does opposing counsel believe that no matter what it takes he/she must win? If the other side believes that whatever it takes to win will be done, then you must act accordingly and temper that behavior.

It may help by speaking plainly with the counsel and highlighting there is a mutual resolution available for all parties. Many parties are blinded by the fight. Do not be blinded by a fight. Always be open to a positive resolution. To look the part, first gain respect.

This is why so many young attorneys believe there is a buddy-buddy system because those older attorneys have worked together and have gained the respect of each other and their peers. Young attorneys can do the same.

Remember, no one is out to get you. In fact, most attorneys want to work with you. But the trust must grow naturally. I really have never found an attorney who utterly dislikes another attorney. If there are non-amicable attorneys, then sometimes it is deserved.

We must always live up to our word. We must always allow a handshake to be a contract. If there is not mutual respect, it is difficult to believe another attorney's position or posture. We must always live up to our morals. If we cannot live up to our morals, no matter the conduct of the other party, then we are not ethical enough to be in the profession to begin with. Our actions should not be based on anyone else's actions other than ourselves. If we do not believe strongly enough in our morals and what we do and who we are, then quite honestly, we should not be in the profession. We do not have the moral gumption or ability to do what needs to be done ethically in a stressful situation.

Nothing you do should be based upon the actions of anyone else. Do not believe you must act a certain way because someone else is acting a certain way. Do not believe that you must do something because someone else is doing something. Only do what you believe is right based on your morals, principles, and ethics. Do not do something because another attorney told you to do it or is doing it. Honestly, do not do something because your client told you to do it. If it is wrong, it is wrong.

This is the same with opposing counsel. Do not treat the opposition the way they are treating you. Treat them the way others in the profession would want to be treated. Treat them how you would want to be treated. Live by the Golden Rule and look the part; act the part; be the attorney you would look up to. Be the attorney others would look up to. Whether you like it or not, you are a role model. Simply being an attorney makes you a role model. You accepted the role of modeling the law, and that is the definition of a role model.

Ask yourself, are you the definition of the law you want to emulate? Are you the definition of what the Constitution stands for, or are you contrary to what we want modeled as the law?

We must be role models for those around us, our teams, our clients, other counsel, and society in general. Be whom you want to be. Do not be afraid to stand up for what is right. Do not be afraid to spend many hours for little pay, doing what is mandated by society and by the law. That is the duty of what you have signed up for. Do not allow the opposing counsel to hamper your ability to see clearly.

In a deposition, handle your position with civil discourse and with the proper amount of confidence. Do not allow someone else to persuade you that you are wrong if you know you are right, but at the same time, be open-minded to a situation. Understand you have more of a unique perspective than that person does. If you listen more than you talk, many times you will come out ahead.

At the same time, do not be afraid to stand up and fight if your client needs to be defended. It is okay to stand up and assert the rightfulness of what you and your client are or have done. In trial, deposition, or mediation, have confidence but not insolence. Look the others in the eye and tell the truth, which will lead to the justice that society demands and the art of law requires. Put on your suit. Put on your tie. Look the part. Act the part. Your client does not come to the law office to find someone in jeans and a t-shirt. Be ready to go to court in five minutes, and you will look appropriate. If you cannot be ready to go to court in five minutes, then you clearly are not ready to litigate. No client wants a litigation attorney who is unwilling to go to court.

If you do not want to go to court, the best solution is to find a resolution good for everyone. But you must be willing to put up the fight if the time, the client, and the facts demand it. Pick up the phone, talk to opposing counsel, email them with respect, be friendly with them, but understand they are still your opposing counsel. Speak with them about terms that benefit you and your case — sometimes that is admitting weaknesses. By admitting weaknesses, you can create a level of discussion that shows the opposing counsel you are not blind to the issues. You believe you can overcome those issues the other side may be leaning on. Many times, parties, including yourself, believe others see what they want to see.

Everyone sees it; everyone has the same training, the same books, the same laws, and the same facts. Everyone sees it; he/she just have separate opinions and perceptions of the situation. Admit the issues; admit the strengths. Find a resolution. Be friendly, but be willing to fight with the opposing counsel should the time come.

Chapter VIII
The Art of Knowing the Decision Makers

"Law is order, and good law is good order."

— Aristotle

Some of the most important people to understand are the judges. However, we have mediators, guardian ad litems, and at times, justices. All these are impartial roles but make decisions. Many people say some of these people do not make decisions. Do not be fooled; each one is a decision maker. Understanding them and understanding that what

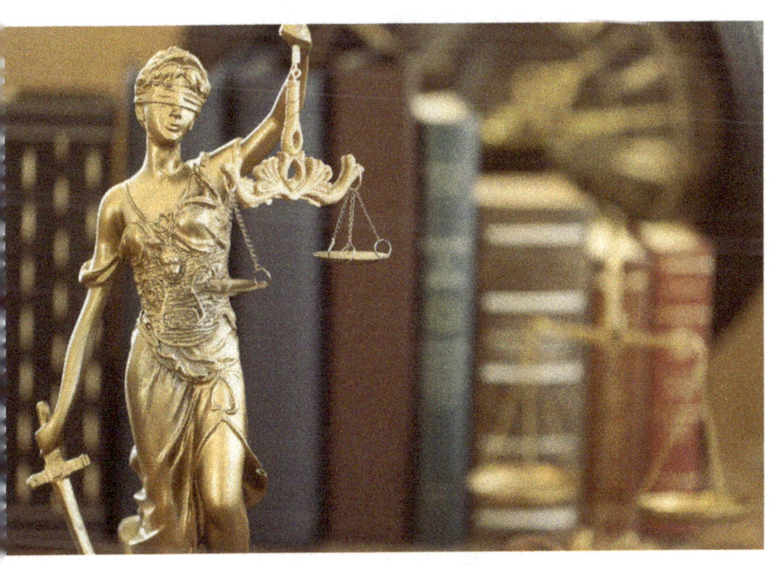

they are looking for is crucial to understand the value of the picture being painted.

For example, before becoming a judge, each person grew up in a certain type of household and received a certain type of education. Before becoming a justice, each had a job. Now, if someone told you the judge hearing a dog bite case had been a dog catcher prior to becoming a judge, would you believe the judge would be more partial? How about if the judge was affiliated with PETA? Do you think the judge might rule differently?

Consider the partialities that might exist among the following hypotheticals

- a land dispute between a mediator who was a surveyor and someone who was an environmentalist.
- guardian ad litem, who did not have a family or a person who had an abusive family.
- someone who had appellate experience or someone who had no legal experience on the Supreme Court.

Everybody has a background. Understand that background. Understand that justice, that judge, and that guardian ad litem. Get to know each one intimately. Most likely, you will be seeing them over and over and over again.

Think about guardian ad litems—people who help make decisions for those who are incapable of making decisions for themselves, such as the elderly, the incompetent, or children. Do they have grandparents? Have they lived through a challenging situation with children? Do they have relatives in the legal field?

Understand the persons behind the guardian ad litem label. What are they looking for? Ask other attorneys who have used this person. Many times, you can choose (but do not choose one that is a friend of the opposing counsel) friends, but not someone who finds impartiality difficult. Friends are created by a certain level of trust: trust they have with someone other than you. They will be spoken to on a weekly basis about other stuff, yet somehow the cases and work will always come up. It is not dishonest; it is just because attorneys have two things:

1. They have work.
2. They have more work.

Likewise, with mediators, you should do more listening than talking. In a mediation, everybody understands the facts. Everyone understands the situation, having lived with it for years at that point.

I have always found the best way to work a mediation is simply to summarize and highlight two or three points and take no more than ten to fifteen minutes for an opening statement. That is for the mediator's benefit, as the adjuster understands the situation as does the opposing counsel and party. The attorneys understand the situation. The only persons who do not fully understand the situation are the mediators, who will say their job is simply to try to find a resolution, but will the mediators push one side harder than the other? Will the mediators highlight weaknesses and strengths? Some will; some will not. Those who will are the ones you want to use.

You want mediators to learn your strengths and understand your weaknesses. You want them to push both sides in truth. Ask the mediators what they think about the case. Ask the mediators what seems good, what seems bad, and what they will get out of it. The mediators may not be able to get anything out of it, or maybe they can get a lot out of it. The mediators might see something you do not see. They may need to come in and control your client more than get the situation itself under control.

Some clients are exceedingly difficult to control when they see dollar signs and think their case is worth a million dollars when the first offer is ten dollars, and the case's value is somewhere in between. This is where, hopefully, an impartial mediator can step in and assist the situation.

A judge's job is to rule on the law, not to rule on a case. But inevitably, judges still have opinions, and if judges believe a case is worthless, they will try to find the law that gets rid of that case. They do not want to be affiliated with bad cases, and they do not want to be affiliated with bad results. But what is the definition of bad? That is a perception, and if the judge believes in his or her own perception that the case is bad, he/she will try to rule against that case. Through a motion to dismiss or a summary judgment motion, some sort of motion will be the perfect reason to end a case.

Does the judge have a brother who is a doctor? Well, you might not want to do medical malpractice with that judge. Continue that case if you can until you get another judge. Has that judge had a divorce? Will that judge like or dislike your client? These are all great unknowns unless you have taken the time to truly investigate and understand each of the decision makers in a case. Has that judge had a terrible experience with you and your law firm? Were you unprepared or were you late? Maybe you are appealing that judge.

Judges are people. They have memories. They know, even if they cannot show that they know. And you might not be the one they like, or if they do like you, they may not overtly do you a favor, but they may not go against you either. While another court may rule against you, you can still build leverage with a single victory. You may know you are wrong based on precedent, but by winning or by at least not having that case dismissed at that level, gives you the leverage to try to work it out in the meantime, as long as you do not become too overconfident, believe in your case too strongly, or believe you are invincible.

The same is true for your client. If it does not make it to the appellate court or the Supreme Court, your client needs to understand the role. It is simple to find an argument on whether or not the judge made an error of law. The hard part is proving it because most justices of an appellate court do not want to say the trial judge made an error. But again, they are held to a standard of public policy and perception. Whether they admit it or not, their role as gatekeepers is what they want the law to be in the state or in the country. They dictate the tone and the tenor of the law. Many justices, as we have seen, feel as if the law should stay the same, and many justices believe the law should change with society.

You should strive to understand those justices, the panel on the appellate court, and the panel on the Supreme Court. Understand what they are looking for. Again, they did not become Supreme Court justices when they woke up. They went through a series of life patterns.

- Can you relate to them?
- Can you have them remain interested in your case?
- Can you have them care about your case?
- Are you just another number put in front of them?

Many people get up and argue the case straightforwardly without having to have a personal effect or have it relating to any of the justices or the judges. Just like a jury, have it relate to them; have it impact them directly. Have them view it as a necessity, either because of societal needs or because of personal needs, wishes, or wants. Understand the art of appealing to the decision makers. Understand they are people, and they are not impartial. They may be impartial in their words, but they are not impartial in their emotions and their actions. No matter how much they want to be unbiased, in their minds, they will pick a side. In their minds, they will pick a value in a case.

- Does that justice want abortion to be legal or illegal?
- Does that justice want you to be able to recover a million dollars for hot coffee?
- Does the justice believe it to be frivolous or proper?
- Is it punitive or an accident?
- What is that justice's experience; has he/she actually been in a car accident before to understand the impact a car accident might have on a person or family?
- Has the justice been sued for a car accident and think that it is a waste of time?
- Does the justice think people are litigious?

This is hard to say, but it is the heart of the law. Find a way to relate it to those decision makers.

Chapter IX
The Art of Knowing the Jury

"Discourage litigation. Persuade your neighbor to compromise whenever you can. As a peacemaker, the lawyer has a superior opportunity of being a good man. There will still be business enough."

— Abraham Lincoln

In determining decision makers, everyone would agree that a jury belongs in that category, even though a jury is not a decision maker. Rather, the jury is comprised of multiple

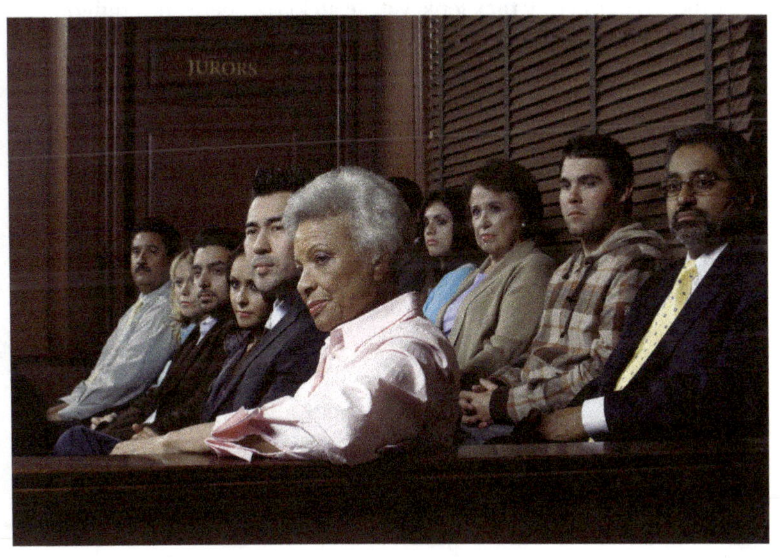

decision makers combined against their will to be decision makers. It is important for you to understand the jury.

Understanding jury theory is a prolific topic in many, many books. The jury truly is the ultimate venue for the art to take place. The jury members are the critics of your artwork. If you were making a dish, they would be the Michelin star judging panel to say whether your dish was good enough to be awarded or not.

But what is it about the jury that makes it an art form? It is looking at the jury and understanding who its core is. Are the members a certain race? A certain gender? Are they dressed a certain way? Do they have jobs, and do they want to miss those jobs? Or do they not want to make a statement by serving on a jury?

We have limited knowledge about jurors' backgrounds other than the way they look, yet we all know there are a million cases about not being able to discriminate against a jury. I am here to tell you that you must discriminate against a jury. You must discriminate against how they will think. How they will act. How do they act based on their leanings? Do you really want to have a juror (if you are the plaintiff) who does not want to be there and who wants to leave as soon as possible? The easiest verdict is just to say no and move on. But for a defense counsel that is perfect, do you really want a jury of people to serve on a criminal charge who look like they woke up high on drugs that morning? Do you want a bunch of executives who have a lot of money to serve on a car accident situation where they feel like it is just a frivolous lawsuit, and you are wasting their time? These are the perceptions you must look and listen for when you have a jury of twelve: the attitudes, the behaviors, the words spoken, the actions taken and not taken.

Most of the time, the worst thing that can happen is a hung jury or a mistrial because the last thing you want to do is try it again. If you do not have the proper understanding of your jurors, then you will not have a proper return on your investment. By the time you get to the jury, you could have anywhere from twenty-five thousand dollars to a million dollars accumulated in cost. Do you really want to have to do that again?

- Determine the level of importance for the case.
- Do they relate to your client?
- Do they relate to the other side?
- Do they appreciate you and what you had to go through?
- Can you tell them a story?
- Do they want to hear your story, or do they just want to go home?
- Do they care enough to be invested in the case or do they not care enough? Did they just roll out of bed and came to court because they get free lunch?
- Have they ever gotten arrested?
- Are they taking prescription drugs for pain?
- Are they taking illegal drugs?
- What is their history and background?

Everyone knows there are multiple books written about juries, but the ultimate art of the law is understanding the people in their core. You need an understanding of who you are as an artist. Understand the picture you are painting. Be able to persuade the critics of your picture. It is a good picture. It has worth. Those critics are the jury, so you must create value for it. That is the art of the law. You can take what many would believe to be nothing and add value to it by understanding not the law but understanding all the things that go around the law like the heart of the jury. The jury does not care about your law—they care about your story if it creates a connection to your situation and client.

Chapter X
The Art

"It is a pleasant world we live in, sir, a very pleasant world. There are bad people in it, Mr. Richard, but if there were no bad people, there would be no good lawyers."

—Charles Dickens, *The Old Curiosity Shop*

Anyone who went to law school knows the law. Anyone who has passed the bar has studied the past and understands the cases and opinions in the law. Anyone who is a judge, justice, paralegal, or another attorney knows the law. What do you

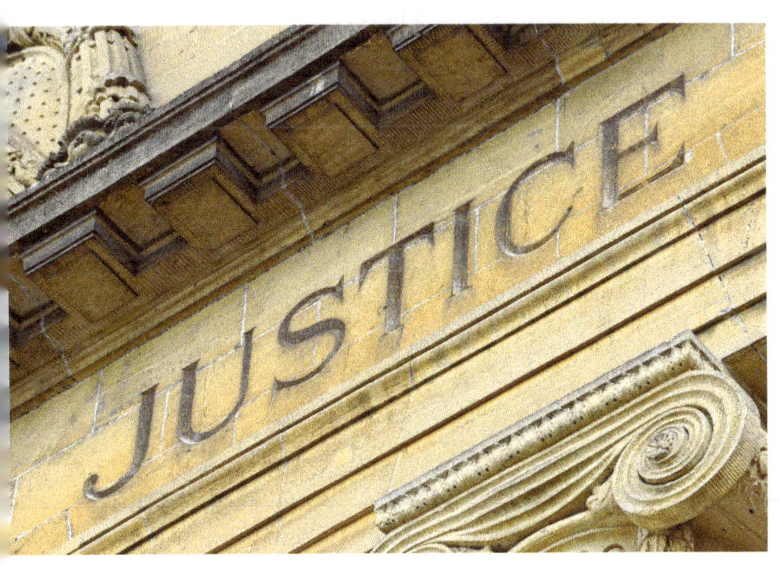

do to change the perceptions of the law in the community around you and for your clients? Can you be open-minded enough to listen to other perceptions of law? What can you do to add diversity to your mentality and to open the door for other beliefs and other perceptions of what is occurring?

These are the benefits of understanding those in the law:

- Gather perceptions on the same facts.
- Leave preconceptions behind.
- Be open-minded for the benefit of others by creating diversity of mind, diversity of thought, and diversity of speech to allow other parties to infiltrate what we have to say and then phrase it in a way that behooves us in our storytelling.
- Always tell the facts of a story and avoid opinions.
- Always be honest with those around you, including your client and including yourself.
- Be confident, not overconfident.
- Have enough confidence in yourself that you are not allowing others to change who you are.
- Understand who you are.
- Understand what you do and why you do it.
- If you do not understand who, what, where, and when, you will burn out sooner rather than later.

It is the goal of an attorney to find an outlet that benefits society and that does not harm himself/herself. Too many people take the term practice of law and believe they can never get it right. That is simply wrong. Understanding the law may be practice, but the people involved are art, and what you do to relate to them is to your benefit. You can paint a picture that you believe is beautiful, and as long as you believe it is beautiful, it is, even though you might have critics who say you are wrong. Sometimes you have situations where you lose, but you still need to do the best job you can. You work hard on that picture and to your client that is valuable; to yourself that should be valuable; to your team that should be valuable; and to the judges, justices, mediators, and the guardian ad litem who saw the facts you were dealt and what you did with those facts is valuable.

The facts are the facts, but what you do with them adds credence and respectability. If you always take cases you know you can win easily, you are simply a dealer of cherries because all you do is cherry pick. But if you are one who is willing to work hard for your client because it is the right thing to do for society and your client, then that is a true attorney and one others will respect. The Constitution and the Bible demand we treat others how we want to be treated. Understand this Golden Rule while you are working the room (they should be working you as well). The art comes in when you work the room harder and better than the other people around you. The law will always be changing. This is why the law, itself, and the statutes, themselves, and the cases, themselves, are practiced because once you have mastered it, then it will change again. But the ability to collaborate with people, to read people, and to have people collaborate with you is an art. This is the ability to listen, to garner respect, and to give respect.

Such practice of the art will create a reputation for yourself and the law, which benefits everyone. It benefits not just you or your client, but it also benefits the law as a whole, giving the law back its reputation.

The law used to mean the standard for all people's freedoms, liberties, and abilities. Without the law there is no freedom, no liberty. Without the law there is no United States of America. Stand up! Be proud! Be yourself! Function as if the law means something to you and your client and society.

Be proud to be an attorney and counselor at law!

About the Author
Thomas William Winslow
Attorney at Law

"But his delight is in the law of the Lord; and in his law doth he meditate day and night. And he shall be like a tree planted by the rivers of water, that bringeth forth his fruit in his season; his leaf also shall not wither; and whatsoever he doeth shall prosper."

— Psalm 1:2-3 (NKJV)

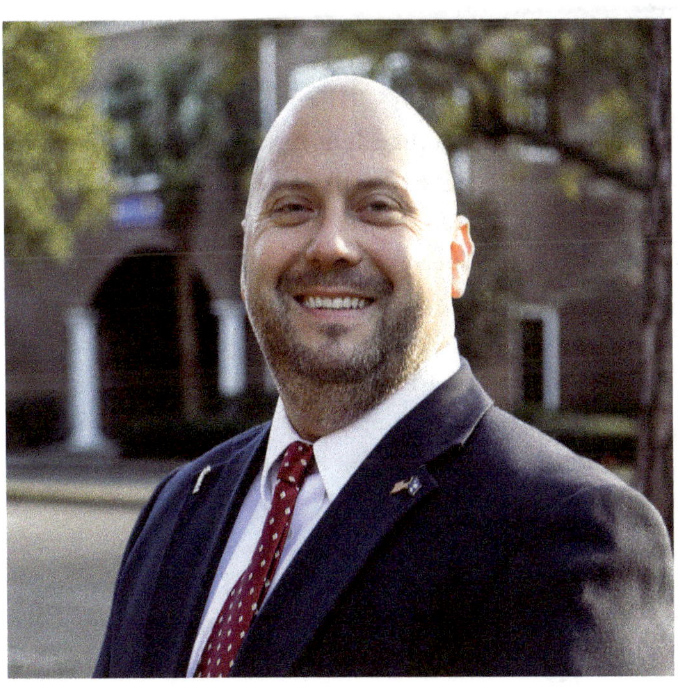

Attorney Thomas W. Winslow is the founding partner of Winslow Law, LLC in Pawleys Island, South Carolina. He has vast experience with medical malpractice and personal injury cases. He has also worked with employment law, family criminal matters, homeowners' associations, police and jail misconduct, maritime law, and products liability. Throughout his practice—whether defending the criminally accused, litigating a contentious claim, or researching and preparing legal documentation—he exhibits an ability to represent clients with the highest degree of competence and professionalism.

Thomas is licensed to practice in state and federal court in South Carolina (Active) and Washington DC (Inactive). This honor allows him access to over seventeen state courts through the reciprocity process. He has also been admitted to practice in Georgia, North Carolina, Pennsylvania, Cherokee Reservation, and Tennessee. Along with practicing law, Thomas is a certified Notary and Mediator in the State of South Carolina. Mediation is a conflict resolution process in which Attorney Winslow helps aggrieved parties settle their differences and resolve disputes.

In high school, Thomas met his wife Lauren, and they quickly became best friends. They married 12 years later in 2006 and moved from Columbia to Georgetown, SC. Lauren was the Parish Administrator at Prince George Winyah Parish Church before deciding to stay at home with their daughter, Lea, and son, William. Together, the Winslows serve their community through many charitable and civic organizations.

Prior to attending Law School, Thomas worked at the National Advocacy Center—the designated training center for all federal prosecutors located in Columbia, South Carolina. Mr. Winslow then earned his law degree from Loyola School of Law and his B.A. in International Studies from the University of South Carolina.

Thomas accepted a partnership with Goldfinch Winslow in 2014. This role allowed him the opportunity to apply his knowledge and experience in helping the people of his community. During this time, Mr. Winslow earned an advanced degree in maritime law from the Charleston School of Law.

In his current work at Winslow Law, LLC, Thomas's involvement with clients often results in a relationship that lasts well beyond the case. He attentively listens and cares about each client.

"We value our clients and our community; that is why we fight for both. Since 2005, I have been helping people and businesses by litigating for those who need an advocate. I have worked on complex litigation with both the plaintiff and the defendant. The practice of law is exciting, and every day motivates me to do the best I can for my clients."

When not at work, Thomas has served as a Board of Director for the Winyah Auditorium, YMCA, SOS, Winyah Gym, Patriots Club, St. Francis Animal Center, Georgetown County Library, and the Tara Hall Home for Boys. He was appointed to the State Pilotage Commission, which governs all the state maritime pilots. Thomas is a Deputy JAG in the South Carolina State Guard. He is a frequent guest speaker, presenter, and lecturer throughout the state. He enjoys the outdoors, skiing, skydiving, cooking, exercising with his wife, and family time with their young daughter and son.

Thomas's children's book, *Firefly Forest*, was recently published and dedicated to his children. It's available wherever you buy books.

66

Lawyer's Oath

I do solemnly swear (or affirm) that: I am duly qualified, according to the Constitution of this State, to exercise the duties of the office to which I have been appointed, and that I will, to the best of my ability, discharge those duties and will preserve, protect and defend the Constitution of this State and of the United States; I will maintain the respect and courtesy due to courts of justice, judicial officers, and those who assist them; To my clients, I pledge faithfulness, competence, diligence, good judgment and prompt communication; To opposing parties and their counsel, I pledge fairness, integrity, and civility, not only in court, but also in all written and oral communications; I will not pursue or maintain any suit or

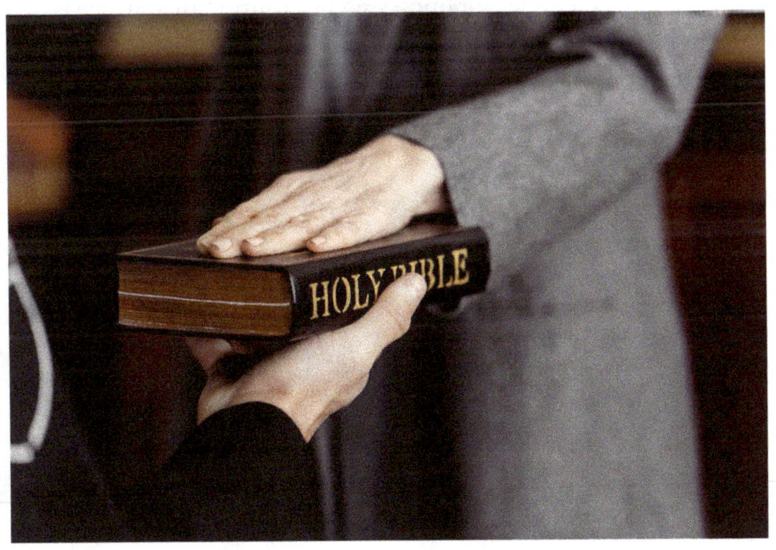

proceeding which appears to me to be unjust nor maintain any defenses except those I believe to be honestly debatable under the law of the land, but this obligation shall not prevent me from defending a person charged with a crime; I will employ for the purpose of maintaining the causes confided to me only such means as are consistent with trust and honor and the principles of professionalism, and will never seek to mislead an opposing party, the judge or jury by a false statement of fact or law; I will respect and preserve inviolate the confidences of my client, and will accept no compensation in connection with a client's business except from the client or with the client's knowledge and approval; I will maintain the dignity of the legal system and advance no fact prejudicial to the honor or reputation of a party or witness, unless required by the justice of the cause with which I am charged; I will assist the defenseless or oppressed by ensuring that justice is available to all citizens and will not delay any person's cause for profit or malice; [So help me God.]

Winslow Law, LLC
Contact Information

e-mail: tom@winslowlawyers.com
Website: www.winslowlawyers.com

Pawleys Island Physical and Mailing Location
11019 Ocean Highway
Pawleys Island, SC 29585
Phone: (843) 357-9301
Fax: (843) 357-9303

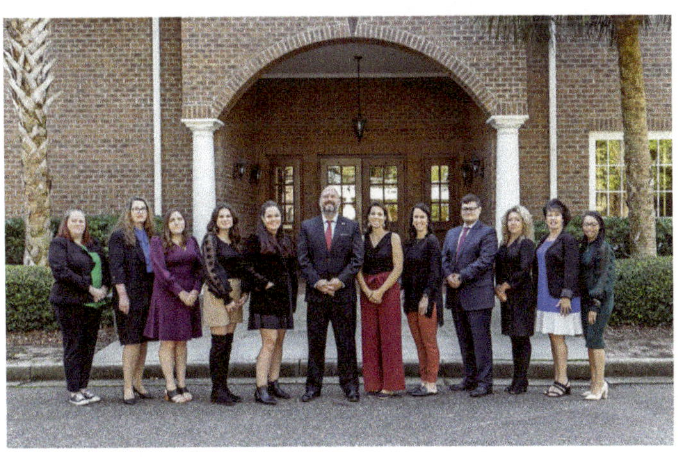

References

Gordon, Leslie A. "Most lawyers are introverted, and that's
    not necessarily a bad thing." *ABA Journal* (January 2016).
    https://www.abajournal.com.

South Carolina Bar. "Lawyer's Oath."
    https://www.scbar.org.

Printed in the USA
CPSIA information can be obtained
at www.ICGtesting.com
LVHW011106080823
754344LV00008B/305/J